POLICY DIALOGUE No. 15

I0103447

THE SAHEL CRISIS AND THE NEED FOR INTERNATIONAL SUPPORT

Author
Morten Bøås

NORDISKA AFRIKAINSITUTET
The Nordic Africa Institute

UPPSALA 2019

INDEXING TERMS:

Conflicts
Crisis
Regional development
International cooperation
Regional security
Political development
Sahel
Mali
Burkina Faso
Niger
Mauritania

The Sahel Crisis and the Need for International Support
NAI Policy Dialogue No 15
Author: Morten Bøås

ISBN 978-91-7106-859-0 print
ISBN 978-91-7106-860-6 pdf

ISSN 1654-9090
eISSN 1654-6709

Language editor: Clive Liddiard
Layout and production editor: Henrik Alfredsson

Front cover: Dogon, Mali, February 2010. Young boy
playing with a tyre. Photo: Mary Newcombe.

THE NORDIC AFRICA INSTITUTE conducts independent,
policy-relevant research, provides analysis and informs
decision-making, with the aim of advancing research-
based knowledge of contemporary Africa. The institute
is jointly financed by the governments of Finland, Iceland
and Sweden.

The opinions expressed in this volume are those of the
author and do not necessarily reflect the views of the
Nordic Africa Institute.

Print editions are available for purchase, more informa-
tion can be found at the NAI web page www.nai.uu.se.

Contents

Mauritania

POPULATION*
3.8 MILLION

- Black Moors (Haratines) 40%
- White Moors (Bidhan) 30%
- Non-Arab Mauritanians (Bambara, Hal-pulaar/Fulbe, Soninké and Wolof) 30%

Muslim **100%**

(Ofiicial)

Mali

POPULATION*
18.4 MILLION

- Bambara 34%
- Fulani (Peuhl) ... 15%
- Sarakole 11%
- Senufo 10%
- Dogon 9%
- Malinke 9%
- Other 12%

(2012-13 estimate)

Other 5%

Muslim **95%**

(2009 estimate)

Burkina Faso

POPULATION*
19.7 MILLION

- Mossi 52%
- Fulani 8%
- Gurma 7%
- Bobo 5%
- Gurunsi 5%
- Senufo 4%
- Other 19%

(2010 estimate)

Traditional 8% Protestant 6%

Roman Catholic 23%

Muslim **62%**

(2010 estimate)

Niger

POPULATION*
19.9 MILLION

- Hausa 53%
- Zarma/ Songhai 21%
- Tuareg 11%
- Fulani (Peuhl) 7%
- Kanuri 6%
- Other 2%

(2006 estimate)

Muslim **99%**

(2012 estimate)

WESTERN SAHARA
ALGERIA
LIBYA
Nouadhibou
MALI
MAURITANIA
Timbuktu Kidal
Agadez
Nouakchott
Konna Niger
NIGER
Mopti Gao
SENEGAL Bamako Djenne Niamey Zinder
CHAD
BURKINA Maradi
Lake Chad
SUDAN
Ouagadougou FASO
GUINEA
Sikasso
SIERRA CÔTE Volta
LEONE D'IVOIRE
NIGERIA
CENTRAL
AFRICAN
REPUBLIC
LIBERIA
CAMEROON
GULF OF GUINEA

Illustration: Henrik Alfredsson, NAI

Mauritania, Mali, Burkina Faso and Niger – four of the Sahel countries.
Statistics source: CIA Fact Book (*Population sizes are July 2018 estimates).

1. Introduction

The Sahel confronts global policymakers with a whole range of serious challenges – fragile states, poverty, refugees and migrants, transnational organised crime (TOC) and jihadist insurgencies. The question of state stability in the Sahel is therefore more prominent on the international agenda than it has ever been, and the magnitude of international assistance and international interventions in various forms is unprecedented.

This is most evident in Mali, but this increased international attention and subsequent turn to military and security approaches to crisis prevention are also present elsewhere in the Sahel. In Mali, the conflict that erupted in 2012 led to military interventions by France (first Operation Serval and later Barkhane), the African Union (AFISMA) and the United Nations (MINUSMA). These various international initiatives have also been supported by the deployment of a European Union (EU) police and rule of law mission (CIVCAP-Sahel) and an EU military training mission in Mali (EUTM).

Despite all these efforts and the signing of a peace agreement for Mali in Algiers in 2015, the situation on the ground has gone from bad to worse. The conflict has spilled over from the north to the central region of the country,[1] and in the first round of the 2018 presidential elections, on 29 July, about 700 polling stations (most in the central region) were closed due to insurgent activities (BBC 2018). Consequently, the most concerned members of the international community fear a spill-over into neighbouring countries, as well. This is evident in Niger, where the US is building a major drone base in Agade and has deployed about 800 Special Forces on the ground. Italy is present with 470 soldiers. There are German troops in the country, and even Norway recently announced that it had entered into an agreement with Niger about a military training mission and had sent a few soldiers to assist in training the Niger army.[2]

There may be good reason for increased military assistance to Mali, Niger and other states in the Sahel. Nonetheless, the question we should ask is not only what external actors believe these countries require, but also what balance there should be between the priorities of external stakeholders and the needs of the inhabitants. Europe wants fewer northbound migrants and refugees, as well as a reduction in what it sees as the terrorist threat; but that may not be the main priority of the people living in the countries in question. Their concern is more immediately tied to living conditions, which have come under immense pressure; meanwhile external interventions have increasingly taken a narrow security approach.[3] This policy dialogue will therefore explore the multidimensional crisis of the Sahel, addressing root causes and showing

---

1   Sangary 2016; Ba and Bøås 2017
2   Bøås 2018
3   Bøås 2018

how this situation has evolved over time. The current crisis is deeply rooted in historical circumstances that external stakeholders cannot ignore. The main area of focus for the policy dialogue is the epicentre of the current conflict, which is located in and around Mali, but which may have several important ramifications for the neighbouring G5 Sahel countries of Burkina Faso, Mauritania and Niger. The security predicament that faces these countries is therefore also explored, and this policy dialogue aims to show that – just as in Mali – external stakeholders there also struggle to find a balance between narrow security concerns and the larger developmental agenda, where military security is but one part of the larger equation.

The Sahel – a multidimensional crisis

The situation in other parts of the Sahel is not yet as dire as it is in Mali, but all states in the region suffer from varying degrees of fragility and weak state capacity. Individually, none of them can respond adequately to the livelihood challenges that currently confront their populations. This situation is further exacerbated by the fact that the Sahel region is in the unfortunate position of consisting of a group of countries that have contributed very little to global CO_2 emissions, but that will be among those worst hit by those emissions. The current projection of an increase in global temperature of two to four degrees will have adverse consequences everywhere; but in the Sahel they will be devastating if those countries do not become more resilient to climate change. If left unaddressed, it constitutes an escalating threat to local livelihoods, with an increased potential for violent conflict between subsistence farmers and pastoralists.

The situation in central Mali illustrates this. Once a commercial hub in the region, Mopti is suffering an economic downturn. Climatic variability impacts on the productive yields of the region, as irregular rainfall leads to low-flooding of the Niger River that reduce the area of cultivable land and agricultural production, making families vulnerable to food insecurity. Pastoralists have become increasingly vulnerable in the wake of successive droughts and poor harvests, which have led to dramatic reductions in herd sizes. The livestock sector throughout West Africa has also been hit by reduced demand and plummeting livestock prices. Thus, compared to other south-central regions (e.g. Bamako, Koulikoro, Sikasso, Kayes and Ségou), Mopti suffers from acute levels of poverty right now, with over 70 per cent of its population living in severe poverty and destitution. In the Mopti area, resource and rights-based conflicts in the Inner Niger Delta are nothing new, but conflicts over disputed access to, and control of, land and water resources are increasing, exacerbated by environmental and demographic pressures.[4]

With resources becoming even scarcer, both new and old cleavages over access to natural resources are increasingly turning violent, as people struggle to control what

---

4   Rupesinghe and Bøås 2018

matters in their lives.[5] This has opened up new scope for violent Islamic insurgencies and transnational organised crime. In peripheral areas of the Sahel, such as northern and central Mali, a void has emerged that neither the Malian state nor international responses have been able to address adequately. This is exacerbated by the multidimensional nature of the crisis of the Sahel: it is about conflict and chronic violence, but it is also a humanitarian crisis caused by a combination of weak statehood and stalled development, and its consequences are human displacement and large-scale migration. The multidimensional features of the crisis confront the international community with huge challenges, as the very weakness of the states in the Sahel means that they lack the institutional response capacity needed to make conventional large-scale external crisis response effective.[6]

In abstract terms, we know what is required: the states of the Sahel need stability, transparency and legitimate institutions that can extract revenues from taxes, fees and duties to deliver economic development and services and to make their countries more resilient to climate-change effects.[7] The problem is how to achieve this in fragmented, conflict-prone societies where the very idea of the state has eroded (if not completely vanished). The challenge is obvious when we consider the track record of the international community in assisting state-building efforts in fragile states. Most often these fall short of their stated objectives; and at times they can even make a difficult situation worse, leaving countries on an international 'artificial life-support system'. This may prevent total state collapse, but it certainly does not represent a sustainable path to recovery, stability, reconciliation and development.

Assistance from the international community to such a process in the Sahel must be knowledge based, and it must be built on a grounded understanding of what these states are and how they work. Unfortunately, a grounded knowledge-based approach is still at odds with the dominant perspective for understanding these challenges, where the states of the Sahel are defined as 'lacking' what modern states are supposed to have: control of their borders, a monopoly on violence, procedures for taxation and dispute settlement, and a legitimate design for transferring power from one ruler or regime to another.[8]

Root causes of conflict

The peripheries of the Sahel are often depicted as ungoverned space – a geographical area characterised by an absence of state control and state sovereignty: a lawless zone, a no-man's land. The implication is that as state capacity has eroded and collapsed, so large parts of the Sahel have turned into an 'ungoverned space' at the mercy of a coalition of forces of transnational crime and global jihad.

---

5   Ba and Bøås 2017
6   Bøås 2017a
7   Fjeldstad et al. 2018
8   Eriksen 2011; Bøås 2015a

However, while few would disagree with the general statement that 'the Malian state is too weak' or would dispute that drugs are trafficked through the Sahel and that forces aligned to global jihad are present in this region, such pronouncements tell us very little about local conflict dynamics. The concern is therefore that these concepts are employed in a way that is less analytical than categorical, leading to a narrow, checklist approach to policy that may result in extremely misguided planning and interventions.

There is no doubt that illicit goods are transported across the Sahel. This is criminal activity. There is also a wide range of political and social resistance in the area – some of it peaceful, some less so. Some resistance is of secular origin, some is religious; and some of the groups are also involved in the transport and protection of the routes used to traffic illicit goods. Some of those involved in this shady business are out to make a profit, while others do it mainly to fund resistance projects. However, many are engaged in various minor roles in the smuggling operations and resistance projects as a coping strategy. Increased climatic variability and few adequate responses from governments and international organisations mean that people must carve out a livelihood wherever they can; and for some (but not all), participation in trafficking or in an armed group has become a new mode of survival. Thus, what we need to focus much more on is understanding the continuity between the different contours of criminality, coping and resistance, and the subsequent logic behind these activities – a logic quite different from the one toward which an 'ungoverned space' lens directs our analyses and policies.[9]

Regional arrangements – castles in the sand?

The situation in Mali is clearly not improving, and insurgencies are also becoming prevalent in most other Sahel states. The precarious security situation in the region is further exacerbated by the almost total absence of any functional regional arrangement. In contrast to the regional warzone that developed in the Mano River Basin in the late 1990s, in the Sahel there is no regional arrangement like the Economic Community of West African States (ECOWAS) or obvious regional hegemon, such as Nigeria. The few regional arrangements that exist are either dysfunctional or severely hampered in their ability to execute policy by the old rivalry between Algeria and Morocco; and this is not likely to change any time soon.

This is the main reason why France, Germany and the EU are placing considerable emphasis on a new regional arrangement, the G5 Sahel. This new regional body, created by the leaders of Mauritania, Mali, Niger, Chad and Burkina Faso, will formally work to strengthen regional cooperation on security and development, aiming to identify common projects that focus on infrastructure, food security, agriculture and pastoralism, and security – important issues that lie behind the root causes of conflict in the region.

---

9   Bøås 2015b; Raineri and Strazzari 2015

External stakeholders in search of a regional framework have greeted this initiative with considerable interest, and it might become a new functional framework for security and development cooperation in the Sahel. However, if this is to take place, external stakeholders need to realise that a regional arrangement rarely becomes more than the sum of its member states – and the member states in question here are all relatively weak states. Thus, in combination with institutional support to the G5 Sahel, state capacity must also be strengthened in the member countries. This is not impossible, but it will be a slow and difficult process, with several setbacks likely. This is evident from the international community engagement in Mali since 2013.

The danger, however, is not only that the process will be rushed by external stakeholders who want to see swift results on the ground, but also that too much emphasis will be placed on the narrow security parameters of the G5 Sahel Joint Force (FC-G5S) and far too little on the development dimension of the larger G5 Sahel agenda. The outcome of this process is still not entirely clear. However, right now it seems as though those external stakeholders that will have to shoulder most of the costs are mainly interested in the FC-G5S part of the G5 Sahel as an arrangement that can provide more 'boots on the ground'. These 'boots' will focus on the external priorities of improved border control, in order to reduce northbound migration flows and to fight those that the same stakeholders define as jihadist terrorists, and thereby a threat to global security. This will make the Sahel into yet another front in the global war on terror. It is in the light of these external priorities that we should interpret the pledge of half a billion dollars for the FC-G5S. As Carbonnel and Emmott of Reuters reported from the meeting that took place in Brussels on 23 February 2018, 'The European Union which believes training local forces will allow it to avoid risking the lives of its own combat troops, doubled its contribution to 116 million euros.' There is therefore every reason to fear that if this goes through, the G5 Sahel contribution will be framed in the same narrow 'war on terror' approach as other ongoing international initiatives, at the expense of the development agenda of the G5 Sahel – which at least contained some prospect for tackling the real root causes of turmoil in the Sahel. The current European pledge of support for the Sahel through support to the G5 Sahel is in fact a pledge of support for European political stability, and not necessarily a sustainable investment in a peace, reconciliation and development agenda for the Sahel.

Being defined as a 'fragile' state can be a bargaining asset when dealing with international donors

Chapter 2, page 14

Headquarters of the G5-Sahel Joint Force in Mopti, Mali. Photo credit: MINUSMA.

FORCE CONJOINTE
POSTE DE COMMANDEMENT

2. Mali and the Sahel – the epicentre of contemporary African conflict

The geographical focus of this policy dialogue is the Sahel, but some delineation of scope is necessary, as the Sahel is an enormous area, stretching from Mauritania in the west to Ethiopia and Eritrea in the east. In this policy dialogue, we focus exclusively on what historically was known as the Sudan region of the Sahel. In current terms, that means the part of the Sahel that comprises the following countries: Mauritania, Mali, Burkina Faso, Niger, and the southern parts of Algeria and Libya. Here, the main focus will be on the turmoil in Mali; but the spill-over effects to neighbouring countries will also be explained and discussed, and the conflict dynamics identified in Mali will be compared to the situation in the neighbouring countries. The policy dialogue will also include a section focusing on the stability and political situation of Mauritania.

Separating the Sahara in the north from the Sudan Savanna in the south, the name Sahel is derived from the Arabic word sāhil, meaning 'coast' or 'shore'. In ancient times, this was an illustrative term, but it is still an accurate name for this part of the African continent. The fact is that there are two possible ways of interpreting the Sahel–Sahara. We can understand it as a great barrier – something that separates both people and places; or conversely, we can see it as an ocean – an area that can be navigated and traversed if one has the relevant knowledge and means of transportation. The latter is a much more accurate interpretation. This is an issue to which we return when we discuss the routes of informal trade and illicit trafficking that run through the Sahel.

State fragility in the Sahel

Burkina Faso, Mali, Mauritania and Niger are some of the poorest and weakest countries in the world, and the fragility of these states is associated (to varying degrees) with instability, chronic violence, humanitarian crises, and large-scale migration or displacement. This confronts the international community with huge challenges, as the lack of an institutional response capacity in these countries makes it difficult for international interventions to succeed. This is obvious in the case of Mali and points to what we may call the 'fragility dilemma'. This dilemma manifests itself in two different, but related ways.

First, a state as Mali is in desperate need of international assistance. However, it will be difficult to get traditional donor assistance to work effectively there: the institutional and administrative response capacity is low, which means that there is only so much external aid that these countries can effectively absorb. Second, given that these countries are in such need of external assistance, one could be forgiven for thinking that donors should have considerable influence there; but that is not necessarily the case. This is the other dimension of the fragility dilemma. For example, in Mali most donors quickly become frustrated with the government, and government leaders are often heavily criticised by members of the donor community for incompetence, mis-management and for tolerating corruption. However, this does not necessarily lead to anything more than vocal criticism – simply because the donors see no real alternative to the regime in power. What this means in effect is that being defined as a 'fragile' state can be a bargaining asset when dealing with international donors, if they see no clear and credible alternative to those in power and position.[10]

As the policy dialogue proceeds, we first discuss how the multi-dimensional crisis of the Sahel affects the main countries of concern in this policy dialogue. This is important because, while all these states may be weak and are currently defined by the international community as fragile states, their weak statehood manifests itself very differently when faced with the current crisis. Mali may be the country worst affected – and indeed it will constitute a significant part of this section of the policy dialogue. However, in even a seemingly strong state (relative to its Sahel neighbours) like Mauritania, there is a web of underlying issues that may come to constitute drivers of conflict. Burkina Faso – which recently underwent a period of turbulent political transition – is increasingly affected in areas bordering Mali by insurgent groups with ties to similar groups in Mali. Most of the reasons for this are local or national; and in this regard we would caution against taking the view that this is just a spill-over from Mali – it is not.

Niger constitutes another interesting angle: in general terms, Niger shares many of the same characteristics as Mali, but it has shown a much greater level of resilience to violent conflict than has Mali. Niger also has a Tuareg minority; but apart from the period between 2007 and 2009, there has not been any really active violent Tuareg insurgency there. This is worthy of note, and we will return to the issue, since the resilience of Niger needs to be better understood as something that cannot be taken for granted. The question needs at least to be asked whether the current external militarisation of Niger and the Sahel will increase or decrease Niger's resilience.

The country-based briefings that now follow constitute the empirical backbone of the subsequent analysis of cross-cutting issues. The policy dialogue rounds off with a concluding section that also contains some policy recommendations.

Mali

Ranked 179th of 187 countries on the UNDP Human Development Index 2017, Mali is one of the world's poorest countries, where most of the people scrape a living from agriculture and animal husbandry – traditional livelihoods that are threatened both by violence and conflict and by demographic trends. Mali's current population of approximately 18.6 million is projected to increase to over 45 million by 2050. This projection is based on the current annual population growth of over 3 per cent; each woman in Mali gives birth to an average of 6.2 children. Half of the population is below the age of 15, and two out of every three persons in Mali live on less than two dollars a day.[11]

---

10 See also Bøås 2017a
11 World Bank 2016a

This trend is not sustainable in the long run, and its consequences are further exacerbated by the effects of climate change. For Mali, the combined forces of population growth and climate-change effects are reducing the amount of land available for agriculture. Meanwhile, sales of land involving monetary transactions are increasing: most often the land that is sold is not used by the owner, but has been rented out to someone else, who then loses access to the land. The inevitable result is greater competition for land – sometimes (though not necessarily always) violent; the potential is there for land to be appropriated by those who employ force. This is what is taking place in the Inner Niger Delta in central Mali. Traditional arrangements (such as customary tenure regimes) have increasingly become dysfunctional or are simply not able to cope with more and more conflicts, while the apparatus of modern administration (courts, etc.) is scanty and often far away; it is also expensive to use and often riven by corruption and biased mismanagement.

Land-rights conflicts in Mali are nothing new, but their importance as drivers of conflict is clearly rising. The main reason is that land is an existential commodity in a country like Mali. It provides the opportunity for current survival and a guarantee for future coping. If access to land is under threat, it must be protected; and this protection must be sought wherever it can be found – that includes among jihadist insurgents, if no other alternatives are credible or available.[12] Such conflicts can emerge within communities (between different lineages, for example) or between communities with differing preferences for land use (e.g. agriculturalists vs pastoralists). Not all land-rights conflicts in Mali are based on this cleavage; but as more and more land in the Inner Niger Delta and its tributaries is cultivated, so there are fewer corridors available that allow access to water resources for pastoralists and their herds of cattle. Thus, in the Inner Niger Delta we find a multitude of such conflicts, some of them appropriated by jihadist insurgents.

The first evidence came from in and around the town of Konna in 2013, with Fulani herders pitted against local farmers. That same year, there were similar conflicts in the Gao area involving Fulani and Tuareg communities, where the former gained the support of the Movement for Unity and Jihad in West Africa (MUJAO). This conflict is currently ongoing in parts of the delta, where local land-rights conflicts have been appropriated by the Fulani-based Macina Liberation Front (FLM). We return to the situation in the Inner Niger Delta of Mali later in the policy dialogue, when we discuss the cross-cutting issue of land rights and the crisis of pastoralism in the Sahel; here let it be noted that even if we see land-rights conflicts and their appropriation by violent entrepreneurs as a major driver of violence, we take issue with how this is framed in the anti-terror framework that has become the hallmark of international operations in Mali – and increasingly also elsewhere in the Sahel.

After the failed attempt in early January 2013 by ECOWAS and the African Union (AU) to respond to the Malian crisis, France launched a military operation, Operation Serval, following a request from the transitional authorities in Bamako. This was

---

12   Bøås and Dunn 2013

followed by the AU operation, AFISMA. Operation Serval succeeded in pushing the jihadist insurgents out of the main northern cities of Gao, Kidal and Timbuktu. However, reluctant to take formal 'ownership' of the international engagement in Mali, yet also concerned that AFISMA would not be able to sustain Serval's military gains, France insisted on a stronger multilateral arrangement.[13] France wanted AFISMA to be converted into a UN force, like MINUSMA. That would also enable France to wield considerable influence over MINUSMA, while the costs could be more widely distributed. All this was possible because France holds a permanent seat on the UN Security Council, from where it was responsible for drafting resolutions on MINUS-MA.[14] When Operation Serval was replaced by Operation Barkhane in July 2014, the scope of the French mission expanded to include other former French colonies in the region – Burkina Faso, Chad, Mauritania and Niger. Thus, even if Barkhane represented a wider geographical focus, it also reinforced the anti-terror approach to the Malian crisis, an approach that has been strongly promoted by French security and foreign politics.[15] This policy dialogue takes issue not with the (obvious) need for a military approach to insurgencies such as Mokhtar Belmokhtar's al-Mourabitoun, but with the fact that the Malian crisis has been framed within such a narrow focus. This has come to inform how the Malian state, opposition groups, other political actors on the ground and the external stakeholder approach the crisis and the issues at stake. This is particularly pertinent in the case of the government in Bamako, as having the crisis defined as one caused by foreign terrorist insurgencies provides a convenient excuse for not dealing with the underlying internal causes of conflict and the drivers of violence. As the crisis that erupted in Mali in 2012 is ongoing and is increasingly taking a turn for the worse, there is an obvious need to recalibrate current approaches. This should be done with an eye to the historical context, as it is impossible to make sense of the current situation without an understanding of the past.

Understanding Mali: a narrative of people, place and space

Modern Mali is based on the legacy of ancient civilisations with vast empires (Wagadou, Mande and Songhay) and kingdoms (the Fulani of Macina, Kenedougou, Khassonke and Kaarta). Islam arrived in Mali around the ninth century, and the great cities of ancient Mali – like Timbuktu, Gao and Djenne – became famous throughout the Islamic world for their wealth and scholarship. However, these vast empires eventually fractured into various smaller states. Not much was left of the former glory when the French colonial powers arrived in the late nineteenth century.

In the 1990s, Mali was portrayed as the beacon of neoliberal democratisation in West Africa. However, behind what was presented as a showcase of democracy, good governance, peace and reconciliation lay institutional weakness, mismanagement and collusion involving regional and national elite interests that paid scant attention to

---

13 Théroux-Benoni 2014
14 Tardy 2016
15 Marchal 2013

human security and development. When the current crisis broke in 2012, Mali was a weak and fragile state with hardly any formal institutions or networks capable of working out sustainable compromises at the local level. It was a multiparty democracy; but as every political party was sustained by a vertical hierarchy of patronage networks, the resilience of the political system was very low, as was shown by the March 2012 coup. This weakness and fragility remain evident in the capital region, but even more so in the peripheral border regions of northern and central Mali. It is a long way from Bamako in the southwest to Kidal in the northeast, and the implications of this centre–periphery relationship need to be recognised. Furthermore, it is important to acknowledge that Mali shares with the other francophone countries of West Africa a tradition of centralised government that is not easily reformed or altered. This is a tradition that tends to prevail despite the weakness of the state.

The first decades

When Mali gained independence in 1960, President Modibo Keita established a series of state corporations. However, apart from those in the cotton sector, all proved to be inefficient, money-wasting enterprises. Other ambitious efforts to create a state-centred economy also foundered, and in 1968 Keita was overthrown in an army coup led by Moussa Traoré. Under his rule, Mali continued to experiment with Soviet-style socialism, but the economic benefits failed to materialise – aside from the spoils that the new elite kept for themselves. Aid funding disappeared into the pockets of military officers, high-ranking civil servants and politicians, with the president himself one of the main culprits. The country was marked by corruption and impunity for the elite and the well-connected few.[16]

When the economy fell into serious recession in the 1980s, a process of economic liberalisation was finally initiated. However, it was too late to save the old regime: it had become increasingly clear that Traoré's system of patronage could no longer be financed, and the voices of the political opposition came to be raised in favour of deeper political reforms. In March 1991, a peaceful pro-democracy demonstration in Bamako attracted a crowd of about 30,000 people and brought together various political activists and organisations. The protest was peaceful, but still security forces opened fire on the protestors. After three days of unrest, the army, led by General Amadou Toumani Touré (aka ATT) overthrew Moussa Traoré and assumed power. However, although this led to multiparty democracy, it failed to change the logic of neopatrimonial politics fundamentally.

A year later, General Touré resigned, in line with his pledge to arrange multiparty elections. These were held in June 1992 and were won by Alpha Oumar Konaré and his party the Alliance for Democracy in Mali (ADEMA). In 1997, he was re-elected for a second term, but this time the elections were marred by irregularities and the withdrawal of opposition parties from the electoral process. Voter turnout was also very

---

16   Bratton et al. 2002; Hesseling and van Dijk 2005

low: only 21.6 per cent in the general elections and 28.4 per cent in the presidential election. In 2002, Konaré demonstrated his loyalty to the new constitution established during his time in office and stepped down after two terms as president. In April of that year, ATT – now a civilian – was duly elected president.

These important changes were part of a process that was largely initiated and driven from the south – the capital region in particular. Even in the peace process and the integration that was supposed to follow, most of the Tuareg population remained on the margins. This was evident in all three Tuareg regions – Timbuktu, Gao and Kidal – but was most explicitly felt in Kidal, due to its isolation from the rest of the country. In many ways, the state of Mali still ends where the road ends in Gao. Kidal is somewhere else – neither in Mali nor in any other country: it is somewhere in between, a hinterland in limbo between Algeria and Mali.

The Tuareg minority: a history of withdrawal, resistance and separatism as an alias

Mali is an ethnically diverse country. The majority groups belong to the Mande superstructure: these are the ethnic groups of Bambara, Malinke and Soninke, which comprise about half of the population. Another 17 per cent are Fulani (or Peul); 12 per cent Voltaic; 6 per cent Songhay; about 3 per cent Tuareg; and a further 5 per cent are classified as 'other' – these include the Arab or Moorish population living in the north. All these groups have their own traditions, politics and language; but the main dividing line has historically been between the Tuareg and Arab population in the northernmost part of the country and the black majority groups, most of whom live south of the Niger River.

Northern Mali – the home of the country's Tuareg minority – comprises the broad part of the Sahara that borders Algeria, Burkina Faso, Mauritania and Niger. Resisting external intervention in their traditional livelihood of nomadic pastoralism, the Tuareg have fought several wars for autonomy – both during and after colonialism. Today, northern Mali may seem like an isolated and forlorn place at the end of the universe. However, it was once an important frontier region, well integrated into the global economy; in fact, a similar process has been taking place recently – now through the economic power of the illicit world of trafficking in contraband, migrants and narcotics. Thus, to a certain extent, the current increase in informal and/or illicit trade can also be said to represent a revitalisation of the ancient routes of trade, commerce and pilgrimage that passed through this area and that connected West Africa to the Mediterranean and to the Middle East and the Persian Gulf.[17]

The position of the Tuareg in the northern region was turned upside down by French colonialism and this was made permanent by the post-colonial state system. The Tuareg, who had once seen themselves as 'masters of the desert', now suddenly became a tiny minority ruled over by the black population, against whom they had

---

17   Bøås 2012

previously directed their slaving raids. Of Mali's eight regions, the Tuareg today constitute a majority only in Kidal.

The Tuareg are generally seen as 'different' in Mali – and indeed, they consider themselves distinct from the other groups that constitute the Malian polity, differing from them in language, lifestyle and heritage.[18] The Tuareg 'problem' – like the Kurdish 'issue' – is something of a Gordian knot.[19] Ever since Mali became independent, the Tuareg have rebelled against the state – first in the early 1960s and then in the early 1990s.[20] As the National Pact of 1992 failed to produce tangible results on the ground, a new rebellion emerged in 2006.[21] It was relatively small – until many Tuareg returned from post-Gaddafi Libya with masses of arms. This lent fresh impetus to the idea of rebellion, and a new movement was formed, the National Movement for the Liberation of Azawad (MNLA). Whereas Tuareg independence and nationalism had been more of an excuse for previous rebellions, the MNLA declared full independence of Azawad from Mali. No longer was the goal to enter the Malian state and secure positions of power and privilege for Tuareg leaders and leading lineages, but rather to break away from that state.

However, the little that may have existed of Tuareg unity quickly evaporated. As MNLA fighters looted and plundered in the north and the Malian army ran away and engineered the 21 March coup in Bamako, the MNLA was effectively side-lined by other forces: the Tuareg Islamist organisation Ansar ed-Dine, led by Iyad Ag Ghaly, a veteran Tuareg fighter from the 1990s, and two other regional movements – al-Qaeda in the Islamic Maghreb (AQIM) and MUJAO. The latter two are not Tuareg movements per se, but they have been present in the area since around 1998, and so they should not be seen solely as alien invading forces. In fact, they have achieved considerable local integration in certain places and among certain communities in the north, skilfully appropriating local grievances. Today AQIM and MUJAO have become integral parts of the conflict mosaic of northern Mali.[22]

2012: The year of violent transformation

In early 2012, Mali was heading for a new general election and a new president. As this was all taking place in a period of increasing domestic uncertainty and regional instability, the MNLA and other insurgents (jihadists among them) may have viewed this as the strategic moment to start a larger and more ambitious insurgency. It started with the MNLA, but the Islamist movements soon managed to turn the initial Tuareg rebellion onto a different path, through a process that unfolded in four distinct but partly overlapping phases.

The first phase was the period from the establishment of the National Movement of Azawad (MNA) in Timbuktu in November 2010 to the MNLA's first attacks in

---

18 Seely 2001
19 Bøås 2015b
20 Berge 2002
21 Bøås 2012
22 Bøås and Torheim 2013; Bøås 2015b; Raineri and Strazzari 2015

northern Mali in mid-January 2012. Key events include the return of former rebel commander Ibrahim Ag Bahanga to northern Mali in January 2011 after two years of exile in Libya; his subsequent death on 26 August 2011; the Libyan civil war; the return of former Tuareg rebels from Libya to Mali; and the creation of the MNLA in a merger between the MNA and Ag Bahanga's group, the National Alliance of the Tuareg of Mali.

The second phase was the period between mid-January 2012 and the MNLA's declaration of independence for northern Mali as 'Azawad' on 6 April 2012. In this period, the MNLA, in collaboration with the Tuareg-led (Iyad Ag Ghaly) Islamist group Ansar ed-Dine, drove the Malian army out of the northern cities. These military defeats led to protests by the families of military personnel in southern Mali in February, followed by an army mutiny that culminated in the coup of 21 March which removed President Touré from power and installed the National Committee for Recovering Democracy and Restoring the State (CNRDRE) in power. The CNRDRE was chaired by Captain Amadou Haya Sanogo.

With the third phase (6 April 2012 to 8 January 2013), the main point to note is how the Islamist coalition in northern Mali (Ansar ed-Dine, AQIM and MUJAO) politically and militarily outmanoeuvred the MNLA and took control of all major cities in the north. This period ended with the advance of Islamist fighters south of the Niger River into the Mopti region and their seizure of the town of Konna, whereupon the political elite in Bamako turned to French President Hollande for military assistance.

In the fourth phase (8 January to 11 August 2013), the Islamist advance south of the Niger River triggered the French military intervention in Mali, Operation Serval. Together with troops from Chad, other neighbouring countries and some units of the Malian army, the French forces chased the Islamists out of the main towns of the north. They also attempted to gain control of the rest of the north as well, but with little success – in fact, it can be argued that even today the combined French troops, UN soldiers and Malian army have only nominal day-time control of Gao, Kidal and Timbuktu; otherwise the territory of the north is hotly contested. However, the French intervention did succeed in creating enough stability for Mali to hold democratic presidential elections, culminating in the second round of presidential elections on 11 August 2013, won by Ibrahim Boubacar Keita – with 77.6 per cent of the vote, against Soumaila Cissé's 22.4 per cent. The elections returned Mali to a nominal form of political stability, but President Keita's public approval ratings have since plummeted. The main reason is his failure to broker a credible and sustainable peace agreement with the MNLA and to tackle the endemic corruption that has continued unabated, despite his election promise to clean up the political-administrative system.

Whereas the 2013 elections took place in a relatively upbeat and positive atmosphere, that was not the case in the summer 2018 presidential elections. Over 20 candidates participated, but the population at large seemed little interested in the elections. There was not much of an election campaign, as most of the candidates lacked the funds to run a national campaign and the threat of violence from Salafi insurgents was ever present in the north and the central region. Though the fear of violence was much in evidence, the number of attacks and casualties was lower than expected. In the first round, on Sunday, 29 July, the incumbent, President Ibrahim Boubacar Keita, took 41.4 per cent of the votes. But since 50 per cent plus one vote was required for any candidate to win in the first round, a second round was required. This was held on Sunday, 12 August, when President Keita faced Soumaila Cissé, who had come second in the first round, with 17.8 per cent of the vote. Straight after the result of the first round of voting was released, Cissé – along with third-placed Aliou Boubacar Diallo and fourth-placed Cheick Modibo Diarra – filed a court case ahead of the second round of elections. The case was built on what they claimed were several irregularities, including the allegation that ballot boxes had been stuffed with fake votes. The case was rejected by the court, but what this shows is that the atmosphere during the 2018 elections was very different from that in 2013, when Cissé immediately conceded defeat.

The run-off on 12 August demonstrated how little the Malian population seemed to care about the election and its outcome: less than a quarter of the electorate may have voted. Immediately after the polls closed, the opposition again complained of irregularities, but President Keita (who was expecting to win a second term) dismissed the notion that ballot boxes around the country had been stuffed with votes for him. The international observers – who by and large could only operate (semi)-independently in Bamako and the southern parts of the country – said they would highlight certain irregularities in their reports, but in general they were satisfied with the process.

The international community, and in particular key concerned European stakeholders, may well be satisfied with the outcome: the elections went ahead and they can now claim to be working with a democratically elected Keita government against vicious jihadist insurgents and narco- and human traffickers. Of far more real concern is what it will mean for the whole idea of democracy in Mali if the new Keita administration continues to be more concerned with internal Bamako politics than with making a deliberate attempt to get off the slippery slope to civil war that the country is currently on.

Mauritania

Of the G5 Sahel countries, Mauritania stands out as the strongest. With a population of only about 3.5 million, Mauritania has manoeuvred to become a valuable ally of the West in the fight against Islamic insurgents in the Sahel. Mauritania is mainly a desert country, with approximately 90 per cent of its landmass within the Sahara. The population is accordingly concentrated in the south, where the level of rainfall is slightly higher. On the Atlantic coast, the capital Nouakchott is home to a third of the population. After a period of political instability, with coups d'état in August 2005 and August 2008, the country has had a prolonged period of political stability. The June 2014 presidential election went off peacefully, although the outcome was contested.

However, there are still several critical unresolved political issues to mention, suggesting that even in Mauritania state stability could become a problem.[23] The political

---

23 See also Potter 2018

opposition still complains about the lack of a real democratic space; there are huge social and ethnic cleavages among the population; the issue of slavery has not been completely resolved; youth under-employment is a huge challenge; and the economy is vulnerable to external and internal shocks.

In macro-economic terms, the country is not doing too badly, with per capita gross national income (GNI) of USD 1,270.[24] This is the highest among the G5 Sahel, and is based on the country's wealth of natural resources – particularly in the mining sector, which has experienced growth over several years thanks to a period of high international commodity prices. Mauritania is one of Africa's leading exporters of iron ore, and it also exports gold and copper. It is one of Africa's newest recent oil-producing countries and possesses considerable offshore natural gas deposits. The country's coastal waters and ocean territory also have among the most abundant fish stocks in the world. This is reflected in the EU–Mauritania fisheries agreement, first concluded in 1987. A new protocol, added in May 2016, is the most costly EU protocol on fisheries, with an EU financial contribution of EUR 59,125 million per year.[25]

Despite some years of economic growth, Mauritania's poverty rate remains high, particularly in the rural areas, due to low productivity in the rural sector. Consequently, the country ranks 156th of 188 countries on the United Nations Human Development Index. Other obstacles to poverty reduction include a lack of human capital-intensive sectors, governance issues, the low quality of public services, and a high vulnerability to exogenous shocks. This last feature is best exemplified by the collapse of global iron ore prices in the second half of 2014 and the low oil prices that came about just as the country was expected to start reaping the first significant benefits from oil production. With a reduction of over 10 per cent in mineral production, overall economic activity slowed down in 2015, and real growth fell to 3 per cent of GDP by the end of 2015.

This means that Mauritania today faces several inter-related development challenges: ensuring efficient use of the revenue derived from natural resources, economic diversification and improved governance. The extractive industry, which is the backbone of the economy, creates few jobs. The challenge for the government is to put in place a system of taxation that increases public revenue for productive investments in other sectors of the economy. Most people are employed either in the agricultural or fisheries sectors. However, current productivity levels are low, and these sectors are also very vulnerable to climate change. How climate change will affect Mauritania in the next 30 to 40 years is an issue that must be addressed now, as its future consequences could prove very serious for both human security and state stability. The Mauritanian economy needs to diversify, but this has not yet happened. Rather, the international commodity boom has created even more concentration, with iron ore representing more than 50 per cent of total exports between 2012 and 2013.[26] Diversifying the economy and reducing inequalities are therefore key challenges for Mauritania; but they can only

---

24 World Bank 2016b
25 European Parliament 2016
26 World Bank 2016b

be addressed with a sustained commitment to good governance that includes both economic and political reform.

Traditionally, Mauritania has been much less regionally integrated than its neighbours. It is not a member of the West African Economic and Monetary Union (WAEMU) and it left ECOWAS in 2000 – a move that reflected the Arab identity of the then ruling elite. Mauritania's relatively isolated position in the region has recently been redressed by the country's membership of the G5 Sahel, and the role Mauritania has taken in that group has brought the country much more to the fore in the region. It has contributed to a change in its international status and has led to Mauritania receiving considerably more donor attention; but it has also raised the country's profile regarding regionally oriented Islamic insurgencies, such as AQIM, which may now be more likely to target this country in the Sahel as well.

A divided country

A cursory glance may suggest that Mauritania is much more solid than the rest of the G5 Sahel countries. However, not only does Mauritania inhabit a volatile neighbourhood, but it is also itself a divided country. As one of only two Islamic republics in Africa (the other being the Gambia), its population overwhelmingly shares the same religion of Islam, but they are sharply divided into three distinct ethno-cultural groups. The dominant group, both politically and economically, is made up of the Arab-Berber or Moorish groups/tribes (the 'Bidhan', meaning 'white' or 'light-skinned') that historically pursued a nomadic lifestyle in the northern, central and eastern parts of the country. The Bidhan make up less than a third of the country's population, but they dominate economically and politically. These groups are the descendants of Arab tribes that migrated from the Arabian Peninsula and settled in large areas of northwest Africa. In the area that was to become Mauritania, they intermingled with, and asserted their linguistic and cultural hegemony over, the indigenous Berber groups and converted them to Islam. The new societies that emerged from this encounter engaged in commerce with their black neighbours to the south, but also in wars of enslavement. The society that these groups established is highly hierarchical and tribalised. The Bidhan of Mauritania are organised into about 150 different tribes that are linked by a complex web of social relations, e.g. solidarity, alliances and rivalries.[27] These relations and allegiances to precolonial polities (emirates) and feudal structures remain dominant in all aspects of political and economic life in Mauritania.[28]

The Haratin are probably the largest group in the country, made up of freed (or still enslaved) descendants of black Africans enslaved by the Bidhan. The relationship between the Haratin and the Bidhan is complicated,[29] as the Haratin share the same language, Arab-Muslim culture and social organisation as their (former) masters, the Bidhan. However, this started to change in the late 1970s, with the emergence of

---

27   Marchesin 1992
28   N'Diaye 2006
29   McDougall 2005

a Haratin political movement called El Hor (meaning 'freeman'). This was the first manifestation of the Haratin as an autonomous political and social force. The most important issue for the Haratin has been the fight against the persistence of slavery, but their organisations also demand a political space that befits their actual demographic weight. Progress has been made in the fight against formal slavery, but the Haratin are still by and large an economic underclass that falls far short of being fully represented in local and national politics.

The third group in the country are the West Africans or black Mauritanians. This group constitutes about 30 per cent of the population and comprises four black ethnic groups: the Bambara, the Halpulaar (Fulbe), the Soninké and the Wolof. Mauritania's post-independence history is marked by repeated attempts by this group to assert its non-Arab identity and to claim a more equitable share of political and economic power. Its claims have been met by the Bidhan-dominated state with a combination of repression and co-optation.

The tension that these divisions create is a problem, but they can also be appropriated by Islamic insurgents in the region. Groups like AQIM and Mokhtar Belmokhtar's al-Mourabitoun have Mauritanians among their ranks,[30] and even if Mauritania so far has not been a target for major attacks by these groups, they are present in peripheral areas of the country, where they rest, get supplies, regroup and carry out sporadic attacks.[31] The combination of aggravated economic hardship and intensified tensions between the three dominant ethno-cultural groups of Mauritania could easily lead to an increase in the recruitment of disenfranchised Mauritanian youths into these groups. Particularly at risk are those on the bottom rungs of society, since one of the advantages of the Salafi-inspired insurgent groups is their credo of being 'slaves of God', proposing an egalitarian project where previous social standing (especially slavery related) is not an issue. Clearly, then, there is a need to take seriously AQIM's communique of 8 May 2018, in which it explicitly mentioned Mauritania among the countries that it encouraged its members and supporters to attack.[32]

The political situation

For most of its existence as an independent country, Mauritania was a tightly controlled state that routinely imprisoned opposition figures on various real and trumped-up charges and that made use of regionalism, tribalism and intra-tribe rivalries to divide and rule.[33] However, since the country returned to civilian rule, it looks as though a more positive trend may be about to emerge. The political debate both inside and outside parliament has become more open regarding current political challenges and revisions to the constitution, and it is noteworthy that the current president, Aziz, has decided not to run for a third term (his current mandate ends in 2019).

---

30 Bøås 2015b
31 Vium 2013; Potter 2018
32 Potter 2018
33 N'Diaye 2006

Ethno-cultural cleavages and race issues have been part and parcel of the history of Mauritania – and are still an integral part of the political challenges that the country faces. In 1989, the regime in power took advantage of a border dispute with Senegal to further marginalise black Mauritanians. Many of them suffered ethnic cleansing and large-scale deportations to Senegal and Mali between 1989 and 1992. Some were forced to leave; others fled the country to escape harsh repression; and most of those deported had absolutely no connection to Mali or Senegal. The exact number of deportees will never be known, but the United Nations High Commissioner for Refugees (UNHCR) reported that by 1991 about 53,000 Mauritanians were living in Senegal and at least 13,000 in Mali.[34] The objective was the Arabisation of Mauritania. Between 500 and 600 political prisoners of black Mauritanian origin were executed or tortured to death, and somewhere between 3,000 and 5,000 soldiers and low-ranking civil servants from the same ethnic background were arrested and charged with being involved in attempts to overthrow the government.

During the 1990s, this politics of oppression combined with an element of formal openness (allowing the opposition to field candidates in elections) continued; even then, the Mauritanian government made some attempts to realign itself with the West, by collaborating with the United States in anti-terrorism efforts. Internally, much remained the same. In 2001, the then leading opposition party Action pour le Changement was banned and several of its leaders arrested and put on trial. In June 2003, there was a violent but unsuccessful coup attempt. Though the regime in power managed to conduct another round of elections in November 2003, with President Taya officially re-elected with 67 per cent of the vote, it was increasingly clear that its days were numbered, as the country was caught up in a political and economic impasse. This clearly contributed to a rethinking of the political alignments within the Bidhan elite – not so much to embrace democracy and human and political rights for all citizens of Mauritania, but rather to safeguard their own position as the dominant elite. This is the background to the 2005 and 2008 coups, and subsequent events, with continuous efforts by the Bidhan elite to protect their privileged position, albeit with less violent means than before.

This long period of instability and coups culminated with the election of General Mohamed Ould Abdel Aziz as civilian president on 18 July 2009. He received a 52 per cent majority, but many in the opposition refused to recognise the results, arguing that the elections had been compromised by military junta control; they complained that the international community had sacrificed democracy for presumed state stability. Despite these complaints, the elections were unanimously accepted by Western, Arab and African countries, sanctions were lifted and ordinary formal relations with Aziz's Mauritania were resumed. Aziz went on to win another five-year term in June 2014, with almost 82 per cent of the vote in an election boycotted by sections of the opposition – a boycott which, they hoped, would result in a much lower turnout than the reported 56 per cent.

---

34 UNHCR 1991

Aziz's victory in 2014 was confirmed by Mauritania's highest court. However, there is reason to believe that at least his margin of victory would have been smaller if everybody had had an equal opportunity to vote. This is because the runner-up was the anti-slavery candidate Biram Dah Abeid, who received less than 9 per cent of the vote. As Jeremy Keenan argued in Middle East Eye in June 2014:

> *If all Haratin and blacks were registered on the voters roll, which they are not, and if Mauritanian elections were 100 percent free and fair, which they are not, and if all Haratin-blacks voted on racist-ethnic lines, which is conceivable, then Biram Dah Abeid would be President.*

Mauritania may have entered a new phase of stability with Aziz and the open harassment of the opposition may be a thing of the past. But the question is: how long can this elite continue to re-create itself? What will happen when that is no longer possible? During the first period of Aziz's rule, he was certainly helped by favourable international economic conditions, which, even if wealth was not spread throughout society, did enable the regime to maintain its power base. However, since the end of 2014, this has not been the case anymore, and the regime will have to find an answer.

The next presidential elections are scheduled for 2019. President Aziz has promised not to amend the constitution (which imposes a maximum of two terms) so that he can run for a third term. This is wise and could help to facilitate short- to medium-term stability. In August 2016, Aziz also once more promised to organise political consultations between the different political groups in the country, including the opposition. This process of national dialogue kicked off in October 2016.[35] This is promising, but the question remains unanswered whether the government will be bold enough to embark on wider political and economic reforms that could improve the economy, make it more equitable – and in so doing lay the ground for the forging of a new inclusive social contract built on citizenship, rather than a hierarchy of tribal affiliation.

Burkina Faso

Burkina Faso is another poor landlocked Sahel country with limited natural resources and a relatively weak state. In 2016, its population was estimated at about 18.6 million, with annual growth of 3.1 per cent. Thus it shares with most other countries of the Sahel a population growth rate that is unsustainable, unless the economy starts to grow faster, become more inclusive and climate-change resilient. The challenge is that the economy is still reliant on traditional agriculture, with close to 80 per cent of the population employed in this sector; cotton is the most important cash crop. Gold exports have recently gained in importance, testifying to a diversification (albeit limited) of the economy. This is good, but neither mining nor any other extractive industry can provide a solution to the employment challenge that Burkina Faso – in common with

---

35 AfDB 2016

other Sahel-based countries – is facing. Such sectors can help boost an economy, but the employment effect will remain relatively low.

Burkina Faso's recent political history is the history of a poor country; but it also used to be the story of remarkable political stability. From the coup that led to the death of Thomas Sankara in 1987 to the popular uprising that took place in 2014, Burkina Faso was under the rule of Blaise Compaore. The legacy of Compaore will continue to be debated internally as well as externally, but he was a skilled regional player who managed to keep his country out of conflict. Under his presidency, Burkina Faso avoided being dragged into the wars in the Mano River Basin, and he also managed to keep insurgent groups from targeting the country (by unofficially allowing some of them to use Burkina territory for certain external activities, so long as they did not undertake acts of violence in the country itself). This is not the case anymore, as Burkina Faso faces increasingly frequent attacks in the northern territories, particularly in the areas adjoining Mali. The question is how President Marc Kabore (who won the November 2015 presidential election) and his government will be able to deal with this. This is a particularly pertinent question, as the security apparatus has become increasingly disorganised and fragmented since the departure of Compaore.

Ansarul Islam and the Soum insurgency

In 2012, the eastern part of Gao and Central Mali were home to MUJAO, one of the deadliest groups of Sahel jihadists. However, when French and international forces deployed in Mali in 2013, MUJAO was chased out of Gao and other smaller cities in this area. This brought about a substantial reconfiguration of the jihadist insurgencies in this part of the Sahel. Currently, only remnants of the original MUJAO insurgency exists in the three-state border region – called Liptako-Gourma – dividing central-eastern Mali from Burkina Faso and Niger, but new ones has also been established. These include most notably a group led by Saharawi-born Abou Walid al-Saharawi that has pledged allegiance to Islamic State (IS), and Ansarul Islam that was established by the Burkinabe Ibrahim Malam Dicko.[36]

Dicko is a Fulani, born into a well-known marabout family in Soboulé in Soum province. He studied at various conventional and Koranic schools in Burkina Faso and Mali, and also had a short spell in Niger teaching, before he started to preach in villages in Soum and on two popular local radio stations. His skilful anti-establishment discourse drew a large following throughout Soum province. The radical nature of his speeches caused some alarm, but not much action was taken to prevent them. Dicko was supposedly placed under surveillance by Compaore's security forces; but when the regime fell and its security apparatus fragmented, they lost track of him. What is known is that Dicko was arrested as part of the French Operation Serval in September 2013 in Tessalit, northern Mali, and that he spent some time in prison in Bamako, before being released in 2015. Thereafter, Dicko returned to Soum and Djibo, the

---

36   Strazzari 2018

main town in this part of Burkina Faso. Here, he formed a new group preaching a radical interpretation of Islam. It was this group that gradually morphed into a violent insurgency.[37]

It started with supporters of Dicko violently disrupting rich weddings in Djibo, calling them un-Islamic. This was followed by attacks by Ansarul Islam against schools, threatening – and even killing – teachers who taught in the French language. In November 2016, the conflict escalated to targeted political assassinations of local traditional imams, and larger attacks against military positions in the same area. The Ansarul Islam insurgency is still relatively small; but its connections to Malian Jihadist insurgencies and its ability to appropriate local grievances mean that more sophisticated analysis and policy approaches are required.

The social landscape of an insurgency

If Ansarul Islam is mentioned in international analyses at all, it is most often as a proxy for jihadist insurgencies operating in Mali. It is seen as a Burkinabe offshoot of the Macina Liberation Front (MLF) of Hamadoun Koufa that operates across the border in central Mali. There is no doubt that certain connections exist,[38] but much more important are the popular shared grievances in these two border regions, and the sense of abandonment that people feel. The result is an open void into which such groups can infiltrate, manoeuvre and attempt to organise the social landscape. For want of alternatives, groups like Ansarul Islam are able to attract certain people; this is not (as some observers tend to think) a reaction against modernity, but rather a social response to state practices that are seen as corrupt and a traditional Islam that is seen as perverted. This suggests that an insurgency such as Ansarul Islam is an attempt to create an alternative modernity. It is certainly not a revolt aiming to restore the Macina Empire (of which this area was never part) or the Kingdom of Jelgooji (which never existed as a unified political entity). Many of the underlying causes have nothing directly to do with religion; but the fact that they are branded as religious certainly matters.

The feeling of being abandoned at the very margins of the state is, however, very much present here. Poor infrastructure makes integrated market access difficult. Health centres and schools are few and their quality is low. Water shortages and drought are always an issue, and the mining boom has done nothing to change things to the better: the only thing it has shown the local population is that people whom they consider to be 'foreigners' can exploit the region's resources without bringing any benefits to them. This stands in stark contrast to a social religious entrepreneur as Dicko, who styles himself the 'defender of the poor' and the 'liberator' – somebody who not only takes on the forces of a state that is seen as illegitimate (because it does not care), but who also promises to tackle restrictive social traditions that many young people regard as benefiting only the traditional elite. Much of Dicko's success rests on a discourse that

---

37   ICG 2017
38   Strazzari 2018; Rupesinghe and Bøås 2018

is religious and political at the same time, justifying insurgency and violent revolt with religious narratives, and at the same time promising social emancipation and justice. For some, but clearly not all, this is an attractive political project – one that is seen as better able to deliver than are national governments and their international stakeholders (which are increasingly regarded as irrelevant to the local struggle of people to secure a livelihood that also offers hope for the future). This is the real challenge that a rebellion such as that of Ansarul Islam represents.

Niger

Rated by the UN as one of the least-developed countries in the world, Niger has had a volatile political history, having experienced a number of coups and periods of political instability since it gained independence from France in 1960. After veteran opposition leader Mahamadou Issoufou won the presidential election in March 2011 and gained another term in March 2016, there have been some improvements on the political front that would appear to render Niger far more resilient to conflict than neighbouring Mali. It is true that Niger has shown a higher level of resilience, but this cannot be taken for granted. The country struggles with frequent droughts and widespread poverty, and several insurgencies have also materialised recently. Urged on by Europe, Niger has taken increasingly repressive measures to curb migration and close the migration hubs in the northern parts of the country.

One of the main concerns of Europe and the EU in the Sahel is uncontrolled northbound migration, and the objective of current EU policies is to prevent this as far as possible.[39] It is in this regard that Niger has been singled out – particularly because the town of Agadez has become a main migration hub: in the early 2010s, around 40,000 to 60,000 migrants passed through it annually; in 2016 the figure was over 250,000. According to the International Organization for Migration (IOM), more than half of the migrants who reached Lampedusa had passed through Agadez.[40] In order to prevent this, the EU has taken a number of policy initiatives.

In Niger, the mandate and resources of the EU Common Security and Defence Policy mission, EUCAP Sahel Niger, were strengthened to allow it to work with and support Niger's security forces in cracking down on irregular migration. Basically, this is an attempt to pay Niger to prevent migrants from going further north. In addition, the EU has strongly suggested to the government of Niger to adopt a new law that would criminalise human trafficking, rendering illegal any form of support to cross an international border without legal authorisation and in exchange for money. The law imposes severe penalties, including imprisonment, confiscation of property and removal from public office. In Niamey, this law was quickly passed, without much debate, suggesting that the Niger government was clearly acting under pressure from the EU and important European donor countries. The question that needs to be asked is who actually benefits from this law and this fresh attempt to curb migration by means of a policy of

---

39 Cissé et al. 2017
40 Raineri 2018; Tinti and Westcott 2016

Agadez, Niger, April 11th, 2018. Nigerien soldiers raise the Nigerien and US flags.

securitisation? A survey was conducted by the Danish Demining Group (2014), which asked Niger citizens living in the borderland between Niger, Mali and Burkina Faso to rank the top ten security threats: only 2 per cent mentioned cross-border trade, including human trafficking. What the international community at large may understand as a security risk may therefore be seen locally as just a way of life: a livelihood strategy pursued because of a lack of any other possibilities to earn a living. External security concerns are therefore not necessarily shared by those who live in these areas.

Related to this is Niger's new role as yet another frontier in the 'war on terror' in the Sahel. There is an increased external military presence in Niger, with troops from several European countries, as well as a large US military contingent. This latter was brought to the world's attention when, on 4 October 2017, a convoy of eight vehicles carrying Niger and American Special Forces was ambushed when it left the village of Tongo Tongo. By the time the battle was over, five Niger troops and four Americans were dead.[41] The question is what this new external interest, which emphasises security and military intervention to curb migration and fight insurgencies that are defined as 'Islamic terrorist', means for the future stability of Niger.

Securing Niger – yet another castle in the sand?

Political and social stability is not something that can be taken for granted. Since independence from France in 1958, Niger has lived through a volatile political history. Military regimes and various republics have come and gone, with frequent military coups

41   Penny 2018

and rebellions in the peripheral northern parts of the country. The Tuareg have rebelled on several occasions in the north, and the general lack of livelihood opportunities gives insurgencies the opportunity to recruit among young people, who see little prospect for a better future. In fact, the migration 'industry' that developed around Agadez was one of the few growth sectors in the country that gave people an opportunity to earn some extra money.

Prior to the new European and American focus on Niger (and Agadez in particular), the number of informal 'travel agencies' that offered trips from Agadez to Sebha in Libya soared: from 15 in 2007 to 70 in 2013. Before the crackdown on the migration 'industry' started there were about 100 so-called 'ghettos', offering accommodation to migrants.[42] The result was that for the first time in decades, Agadez became a 'boom' town. This provided extra income not only for its inhabitants, but also for people who came from near and far to take part in the bonanza of the migration 'industry'. It is clearly neither sustainable nor desirable for this to be the future of Agadez and the economic foundation of the town; however, any attempt to dismantle something that provides people who have very little with a bit more must offer those people an economic alternative. If not, the risk is that the ensuing grievances will undermine the fragile social stability that currently exists in Niger.

And that is exactly what has happened. When the new law on trafficking was implemented, some groups were targeted and others were not. Those who remained untouched were those close to the state – what political scientist Luca Raineri identifies as a 'state-sponsored protection racket',[43] in this case the Tuareg elite that controls the administration of Agadez in close connection with Niamey. Meanwhile most of the vehicles confiscated in the clampdown on the migration 'industry' belonged to Tebu traffickers.[44] The Tebu are a small minority group in Niger (constituting less than 0.5 per cent of the population) that has historically been a politically marginalised and economically deprived group. However, this time the group's fortunes had been looking up: thanks to their control of the Tummo border crossing to Libya, they had gained a prominent position in the migration 'industry'.

The Tebu are obviously not happy with the crackdown, and it will only add to the group's already lengthy list of grievances against the state. However, with regard to state stability, a more pertinent question would be what will happen to the current alliance between the president of Niger, Mahamadou Issoufou, and the Tuareg of Agadez. Issoufou's rise to power was supported by several groups, but he forged a particular alliance with the Tuareg elite that controls Agadez – and thereby also a considerable part of the migration industry. The Tuareg elite needed a political patron in Niamey, while Issoufou needed both their political and economic support. But what will happen to this alliance if the president is forced by external stakeholders (like the EU) to limit the activities of traffickers who are part of the state-sponsored protection racket?

---

42   Raineri 2018
43   Raineri 2018: 74
44   Molenaar 2017; Raineri 2018

The situation is further exacerbated by the enhanced US focus on Agadez town and region as yet another hotspot in the 'war on terror.' In the most south-easterly part of Agadez lies what is officially Niger's Air Base 201; but most locals would call it 'the American' base. Officially, it is owned by Niger's military; but for all practical purposes it is paid for, is being built and will be operated by the US military.[45] The air strip will be long enough to handle C-17 transport planes, as well as MQ-9 Reaper drones. As the US is much less concerned about northbound migration than the EU and European countries operating on the ground in Niger, the Agadez base will most likely be used to survey and conduct strikes against Salafi militant groups, such as AQIM, al-Mourabitoun and others.

Viewed from afar, Agadez may seem like peripheral hinterland, lost in time and space. But for such a purpose (as indeed also for irregular migration) the town is perfect. Its location in the wider Sahel region is central. Medium- to long-range drones operating from Agadez could reach all across the Sahel and even large parts of neighbouring Sub-Saharan Africa. From a military point of view, this would give the US Africa Command (AFRICOM) a significant strategic advantage. From the point of view of the regime in Niamey, hosting such a base could also be a good strategic move: it makes the regime a key partner of the US. If necessary, this status could be used to fend off external criticism over democracy, human rights, corruption or other things that development partners sometimes try to intervene in. The Government of Niger also argues that the base will bring development finance to Niger and Agadez.

The question is, how much will actually materialise in local pockets? So far, the most visible local effect has been that the base is on land that formerly belonged to Tuareg cattle-herders. Apart from some small symbolic purchases of local produce, such as fruit and vegetables, it is difficult to imagine that much of what is needed to maintain the base in Agadez will be sourced locally. The bulk of the equipment will come in from abroad, supplied by American companies; meanwhile a few lucky locals may secure some unskilled employment. The base may be able to target insurgents; but as we know from theatres of war elsewhere, drone attacks are rarely quite as targeted as the claims made in official military propaganda. One question that needs to be answered is how the American personnel operating the drones will be able to separate a convoy of insurgents in the desert from an ordinary trading convoy or a migrant-transporting convoy, as those will also be armed: nobody travels unarmed here. Thus, along with the harsher policy on migration that the EU has forced through, the new militarisation of the Sahel that the US is pushing for may end up as yet another 'castle in the sand': it does little to tackle the underlying causes of insurgencies and migration, and may in the long run only further undermine an already immensely fragile social fabric. If that happens, the end result will only be more insurgencies and more northbound migration.

---

45 Penny 2018

This policy dialogue rejects the notion of the Sahel as an 'ungoverned space'.

Chapter 3, page 40

Ansongo, Mali, December 2015. A convoy of French soldiers of the Barkhane military operation. Photo: Fred Marie, Flickr.

3. Conflict trends and drivers of violence

The crisis of the Sahel is multidimensional. Conflict, chronic violence, crime and Salafi-inspired insurgencies are all part of the picture. However, it is all exacerbated by a humanitarian crisis caused by a combination of weak and dysfunctional statehood. The result is stalled development, and its consequences are human displacement and large-scale migration. Conflict in the Sahel is often presented as the outcome of a transnational diffusion of violent Salafi ideology, in combination with transnational crime. While this has become an integral part of the Sahel security predicament, conflict in the Sahel is still deeply locally embedded, and at the heart of the matter are not necessarily issues concerning religion (or any other grand ideology), but land-rights conflicts, which have evolved as a combination of states having lost the capacity to govern and increased pressure on land due to population growth and increased climatic variability.

Land rights and local conflict

Land-rights conflicts in the Sahel are not a new phenomenon, but their importance as drivers of conflict is clearly increasing. The main reason is that land is an existential commodity in any country in the Sahel. It provides current survival as well as being a guarantee for future coping. Thus, if access to land is under threat it must be protected, and this protection must be sought where it can be found – also among jihadist insurgents, if no other alternatives are credible or available.[46] Such conflicts can emerge in communities (between different lineages, for example) or between communities with different preferences for land use, as with agriculturalists vs pastoralists). This is evident in the case of Mali. Not all land-rights conflicts in Mali are based on this cleavage, but as more and more land in the Inner Delta along the Niger River and branch rivers are cultivated, there are fewer corridors available that allow access to water resources for pastoralists and their herds of cattle. Thus, in the Inner Delta along the Niger River we find a multitude of such conflicts, some of them appropriated by jihadist insurgents. Religious ideology obviously also plays a role, but the underlying driver of conflict is land rights. This is not at all unique to Mali and the Inner Delta of the Niger River; the following example is quite typical of how this works in the Sahel at large.

The Mopti region and the Inner Delta of the Niger River have historically been a contested space. The area is rich in resources, but competing systems of governance challenge each other. Those who lose out are the common people of the region. Communal conflict over access to land and water is not new, but is currently being exacerbated by population growth, climate-change effects and armed jihadist groups that

---

46   See also Bøås and Dunn 2013

have developed strategies to appropriate conflicts that a vanishing and dysfunctional state is not able to deal with in a credible and trustworthy manner.

When colonial power arrived in this part of Mali after the fall of the Macina Empire in 1864, the French accepted part of the original management system of natural resources; but they also undermined it through the establishment of a parallel form of land tenure. Customary chiefs managed land under continuous cultivation, while the colonial administration controlled so-called 'unoccupied land' and could grant private property titles. Water and forests were placed under the control of the Water and Forest Agency – the current Direction Nationale des Eaux et Foréts.[47]

It is the increasing corruption and dysfunctionality of these two competing systems of land governance that the MLF is currently preying on: this allows the MLF to use the (increasingly violent) land conflicts to achieve local integration and – if not control of the territory as such – at least a sufficient hold on the population. The MLF has, for example, secured widespread sympathy due to its management and control of the prized bourgoutiéres (the highly nutritious dry-season pastures that pastoralists depend on for livestock grazing), to which it has scrapped access fees, claiming that the land belongs only to 'God'. This is in stark contrast to the rising access fees (sometimes up to CFA 1,000,000) extracted by the 'Jowros', who are part of the noble Rimbe class and the gatekeepers to the pastures. Pasture access fees have fostered huge resentment among herdsmen, who view the Jowros as corrupt and unjust, since they pocket the fees for personal gain.[48] This is but one example from this part of the Sahel to show that while religion is a vector in the current landscape of conflict, the underlying issues are land-rights conflicts. This is what must be managed if the Malian state is to be able once more to assert sovereignty.

Trafficking and organised crime

Besides the role and influence of jihadism, much has also been made of transnational organised crime as an integral part of the conflicts in the Sahel. In line with Bøås (2015b), Raleigh and Dowd (2013) and Strazzari (2014), this policy dialogue rejects the notion of the Sahel as an 'ungoverned space'. In any territory occupied by human beings there will be certain social patterns that are repeated, creating some level of order and trust. This is also the case for the territory of the Sahel, as shown by the informal trade (legal and illicit) that passes through the region. The Sahel – even the peripheral areas – is not without certain levels of order and governance; but these clearly differ from the norms presented in standard political science textbooks.[49] The essential point is the density of the overlapping and competing networks of informal/illicit trade, governance and resistance. These networks are based on personal power, as the 'attainment of big-man status

---

47 Ursu 2018
48 Rupesinghe and Bøås 2018
49 Bøås 2015a

is ... the outcome of a series of acts which elevate a person above the common herd and attract about him a coterie of loyal, lesser men'.[50] These networks vary in depth, geographical reach and their ability to penetrate the states, but all of them are unstable, shifting and constantly adapting; and despite some common interests, their participants do not necessarily share the same goals or have similar reasons for being involved.[51]

The elevation to 'big-man' status in a place like Mali does not follow one universal path. It varies in time and space, and may be based on varying combinations of power. However, as authority is almost always contested, there must be the ability to use force, to generate resources and not least to locate authority in and between the state and the informal. The following thumbnail biographies of three well-known Sahel 'big men' illustrate this point.

Ibrahim Ag Bahanga embarked on his 'big-man' career during the Tuareg rebellion in the 1990s as a lesser rebel leader. He gained control of a commune (division of local government) after the rebellion ended. He was involved in trade and smuggling; he led other rebellions, but also maintained relationships with neighbouring governments in Algeria and Libya, and with segments of the Malian government and administration.

Iyad Ag Ghaly was an important Tuareg rebel commander during the rebellion in the 1990s. He later held various government positions, including at the Malian embassy in Saudi Arabia, but was also involved in minor rebellions together with Ag Bahanga, before he established the Tuareg jihadist insurgency Ansar ed-Dine in 2012.

Mokhtar Belmokhtar is one of the best-known jihadists of the Sahel; but prior to the attack on In Aménas in January 2013, he was better known as a smuggler and kidnapper, with a vast network that must have included actors involved with the forces of transnational crime, as well as operatives of state agencies.

The point about all three men is that their status as 'big men' was not based solely on one aspect of their activities, but on the totality of them – and thereby on their ability to, if not control, then at least influence and maintain partly overlapping networks without a shared view as to long-term objectives and strategy.[52]

Some of these networks and their respective 'big men' are involved in criminal activities mainly to cope with the situation (and hopefully thrive), while others have employed such activities to finance various projects of resistance (secular and religious). This may bring different networks and their 'big men' into conflict with each other; but conflict at one point need not rule out collaboration and collusion in other circumstances. This suggests that a 'nexus' of international crime and terrorism does not exist as a fixed entity, with permanent organisational structures. The logic of these operations and the networks involved is much more one of ambiguity and flexibility, and the actors involved are 'flexians', who adapt themselves and their resources to ever-changing circumstances in the terrain in which they operate.[53]

---

50 Sahlins 1963: 289
51 Bøås 2015a
52 See also Bøås 2017b
53 Wedel 2009; Guichaoua 2011; Debos 2009

Such plasticity is not total, however. Certain relationships and networks are not only more likely than others – they are also more permanent. Ethnicity and kinship may matter, but so do the dangers of certain relationships, no matter how profitable they may be. One example is Mokhtar Belmokhtar. It seems reasonable to suggest that most of his more secular-oriented criminal networks vanished the moment he took responsibility for the In Aménas attack. It was not that it suddenly became less profitable to do business with him – just too dangerous.

The logic of the relationship between criminality, coping and resistance on the Sahel periphery might be described as 'ships that pass in the night'. But certain 'ships' pass each other more frequently than others. Regardless, this leaves us with a scenario where different competing 'big men' vie for the role of nodal points in various networks of informal governance: some mainly profit-driven; others combining income-generating strategies with societal and political objectives (secular and religious); yet others merely seeking to cope (and perhaps thrive in the future). As the constellation of these networks is constantly changing, there is no formal or permanent organisation. This makes it possible to combine various strategies of criminality, coping and resistance without necessarily losing sight of immediate or long-term objectives. The outcome is a narrative-driven space of co-existence, collusion and conflict, in which conflating the interests, ideas and actions of the different actors will only lead to confusion and misguided policies, and not analytical clarity.[54]

Crime and resistance: fractures and continuities

The following example concerning the relationship between the Arab communities of the Kunta and the Tilemsi-Lamhar in Gao and Timbuktu further illustrates the conceptual point made above. In this relationship, the Tilemsi-Lamhar have traditionally been vassals of the Kunta. The Kunta are generally seen as a high-caste tribe, whose political and economic pre-eminence in the region derives from their proclaimed descent from the Prophet and their mastery in religious matters.[55] Historically, the Kunta – an Arab-Moor group claiming to be original descendants of Arabs – were instrumental in the expansion of Islam into Sub-Saharan West Africa in the fifteenth century. They formed an urban elite in Timbuktu, the main city on the southern side of the trans-Saharan trade. In post-colonial Mali, the Kunta have at times come into violent conflict with Tuareg and Bambara populations in towns where they once held a near-monopoly on political power. This happened in 1998/1999, and in 2004 there were also brief outbreaks of inter-communal violence between these groups in Gao and Timbuktu. Similar issues came to the fore when MUJAO took control of Gao in 2012. The Kunta have clashed with majority groups like the Bambara and Tuareg communities, but they have also maintained a relatively solid alliance with the Tuareg Ifoghas of Kidal.

---

54 See also Bøås 2015a; 2015b
55 Scheele 2009

Viewed from this angle, the Kunta–Tilemsi-Lamhar divide is the Arab equivalent of the situation in Kidal between the opposing Tuareg clans of the Ifoghas and Imghad. It is noteworthy that former President Touré actively pursued a policy of seeking to empower the Tilemsi-Lamhar at the expense of the Kunta. Paralleling his approach to the Imghad and the Ifoghas, he turned a blind eye to the growing involvement of the Tilemsi-Lamhar in trafficking activities and drugs smuggling. In consequence, the Kunta and the Ifoghas have often joined forces to defend the status quo in economic power relations in northern Mali.

The Kunta have enjoyed a leading economic position in this area, thanks to their external connections and family networks, which control the cross-border trading routes, particularly towards Algeria. However, as in Kidal, events in the aftermath of the second Tuareg rebellion started to undermine their position: a new wave of discontent with the prevailing social order started to emerge, and if it was not directly hijacked by the political elite in Bamako, attempts were certainly made to manipulate it. This eroded the balance of power and social hierarchy in the Tilemsi Valley of the Gao region, but also cemented the traditional alliance between the Kunta and the Ifoghas. These fractures and alliances became increasingly prominent as larger quantities of valuable contraband were trafficked through these areas.[56] By 2006, control of smuggling routes had come to play an important role in the deepening of pre-existing cleavages. For example, Tilemsi-Lamhar traders and traffickers increasingly preferred the direct route from Gao to the Algerian border town of in-Khalil, in order to avoid the Ifoghas-dominated region of Kidal, now considered 'too expensive' and with too many local fraudsters. The emergence of MUJAO (and their involvement with the association of Arab traders and traffickers from the Tilemsi Valley) is probably also related to the re-emergence and strengthening of this cleavage. It should therefore come as no great surprise that what has been described as the peak of MUJAO fanaticism – the destruction of a Sufi mausoleum 330 km north of Gao, on 15 September 2012 – targeted a symbol-rich place of worship and pilgrimage for the Kunta community.

Unlike other insurgencies operating in northern Mali, MUJAO never offered much political or religious justification for its actions, beyond the pragmatism of what Raineri and Strazzari (2015) call 'jihadism without borders': launching an impressive campaign in favour of traders, traffickers and smugglers, explicitly stating that customs duties, tolls, tariffs and borders were not in accordance with Islamic law and would no longer be enforced. Indeed, when customs duties and taxes were banned, or simply bypassed with the support of MUJAO, living conditions in Gao improved – at least initially. The price of basic commodities – like food and fuel – mainly imported from Algeria dropped significantly. MUJAO and its emir in Gao, Abdel Hakim, soon received the backing of Gao's Cercle des notables, the most widely recognised local representative body. Three local worthies volunteered to act as mediators between MUJAO and the local population: Ali Badi Maiga, Mohamed Baye Maiga and Mohmed Ould Mataly (the first two of Songhay origin, the third a Tilemsi Arab). All were wealthy,

---

56 Bøås 2012

their fortunes allegedly linked to illicit trafficking and criminal activities; but they also needed armed protection under the new circumstances. This was a mutually beneficial arrangement.

The wealth that MUJAO accumulated through its alliance with Gao businessmen facilitated the insurgency's recruitment campaign. MUJAO monthly salaries for young recruits ranged from USD 100 to, in exceptional cases, as much as USD 700: an amount of money that most locals would struggle to earn in a year. 'Easy money' became an important reason for joining the ranks of MUJAO, especially for orphans and the Talibé – boys left to the education and care (mostly through begging) of a local marabout.

This offered MUJAO a sizeable local cohort of young recruits; moreover, because of the underlying religious aspect, it also gave the organisation a reputation as a guardian of morality and legality in social and economic life. This may seem strange, but when compared to the abuse, raids and thefts perpetrated by the MNLA, MUJAO justice seemed preferable to most people in the town. The occasional harshness of MUJAO's sharia was initially seen as nothing compared to the random violence that had reigned in Gao during the nominal rule of the MNLA. Economic activities were especially hit by the uncertainty created by the random violence of the MNLA, so that many businessmen – and not just Arab merchants – concluded that MUJAO's uncompromising mode of law enforcement, including corporal punishment, would at least restore a modicum of order and security that would allow their businesses to operate.

MUJAO also found significant support among some members of Gao's Fulani community. Two competing interpretations have been advanced to explain this collusion. One has focused on long-standing grievances over access to water and pasture land, pitting the Fulani against local Tuareg communities. Fulani collaboration with MUJAO can therefore be interpreted as a form of collective resistance against perceived Tuareg dominance. There is good reason to believe that this was indeed part of the picture, as the area around the city of Gao had long been plagued by local land-rights conflicts. However, other economic issues may also have been at stake. Gao is the Fulani transport hub for northern Mali and beyond. One way of securing local land rights under the new circumstances would be to enter into a security arrangement with MUJAO. In this regard, MUJAO spokesperson Hamadou Ould Kherou's rhetorical turn to such leading figures in the Fulani pantheon as El-Hadji Oumar ibn Said Tall, Ousmane dan Fogo and Amadou Cheikhou can be seen as a means of constructing a discursive bond between the two groups. Once again, these arrangements were to the mutual benefit of both groups, irrespective of the challenges to local peace and stability after MUJAO was chased out of Gao by the French forces.

Beyond the situation in Gao itself and in the areas around the town and the Tilemsi Valley, what this shows is the complex and fractured local nature of the conflict in the Sahel. There is not just one single conflict, but many conflicts that are used, manipulated and conflated by several actors. There is no easy answer to the question of 'who is pulling the strings'. What can be said for certain is that this is not only a game of 'puppet masters': the local 'puppets' also have their own interests and sufficient agency to influence outcomes. Power and authority in the Sahel are full of local complexities that cannot be broken down into neat categories of formal vs informal. The important point is how real authority is located in-between the formal and the informal – those who matter are those who combine positions in the formal and informal structures of the political economy, so that they, as 'big men', become nodal points in 'complex networks of informal governance'. This creates a particular political and social landscape of adaptation and fractures, but also continuities. Certain alliances are ad hoc, in flux and changeable because they are based on short-term opportunism (as between MUJAO and the Cercle des notables in Gao or between MUJAO and parts of the Fulani community in Gao). Others are based on historical alliances of power and economic privilege – like the Kunta–Ifoghas alliances that seek to protect historical control of valuable trade routes.

Niamey, Niger, December 2012. After heavy rains in 2012, the Niger River in flood reached its highest level since 1925, devastating sown fields and houses in the villages and parts of the capital. Photo: Gustave Deghilage, Flickr.

4. Concluding remarks

The crisis in the Sahel is serious and multidimensional, and if it continues unabated it could have consequences far beyond the region. As the states of the region are too poor and weak to deal with this on their own, international support is needed. It is therefore a positive sign that the region of Sahel is higher on the international agenda than it has ever been. The challenge, however, is that current international approaches and interventions in the Sahel are more in line with short-term external priorities, such as stopping irregular migration to Europe and fighting insurgencies that have been defined as part of a global complex of jihadist terrorism. There is no doubt that there is a migration crisis in the Sahel and that it must be addressed. And certainly we do need a military approach to several of the insurgencies. However, it must be part of a much broader agenda of humanitarian assistance and development support that is context and conflict sensitive. Current international approaches – such as the one highlighted in this policy dialogue in Niger – are short-sighted and may, in the end, only undermine the delicate compromise that the current resilience of Niger is built on.

Thus, donors and external stakeholders in need of better partners on the ground have to realise that what is needed is a long-term approach that prioritises state-building over support for the security sector in stopping migration and fighting insurgencies that we define as part of the global war on terror. This is possible, but we also need to acknowledge that the window of opportunity that is currently still available will not stay open for too long. Climate-change effects will manifest themselves in this region, and they will have devastating consequences if the various states' agricultural sectors do not become more climate resilient. This can only happen if the underlying cause of conflict is addressed – and that is not violent jihadism, but the land-rights issue. In this regard, the current international emphasis on the G5 Sahel should change from a focus on more 'boots on the ground' to support for the development agenda of this embryonic international organisation. The Sahel needs a functioning regional framework and the G5 Sahel has some potential; but the only way to harvest this potential is to help fine-tune it to address the underlying causes of conflict. Improving security conditions in the Sahel is absolutely essential; but neither the inhabitants of the region nor the external stakeholders will find security exclusively through military means. The correct priorities must be set. And at the heart of this there must be an improvement in living conditions and a new system of governance that makes it much less possible for jihadist insurgents to appropriate local land-rights conflicts.

References

AfDB (2016) *Republic of Mauritania: Economic Reforms and Diversification Support Programme – Phase I*, Abidjan: AfDB.

Ba, Boubacar and Morten Bøås (2017) *Mali: A political economy analysis*, Oslo: NUPI.

BBC (2018) 'Low turnout in Mali run-off', BBC.com, 13 August.

Berge, Gunvor (2002) 'In Defence of Pastoralism: Form and flux among the Tuareg of northern Mali'. PhD dissertation, Faculty of Social Sciences, University of Oslo.

Bøås, Morten (2012) 'Castles in the sand: informal networks and power brokers in the northern Mali periphery', in Mats Utas (ed.), *African Conflicts and Informal Power: Big men and networks*, London: Zed Books.

Bøås, Morten (2015a) *The Politics of Conflict Economies: Miners, merchants and warriors in the African borderland*, London: Routledge.

Bøås, Morten (2015b) 'Crime, coping and resistance in the Mali-Sahel periphery', *African Security*, vol. 8, no. 4, pp. 299–319.

Bøås, Morten (2017a) 'Fragile states as the new development agenda?', *Forum for Development Studies*, vol. 44, no. 1, pp. 149–54.

Bøås, Morten (2017b) 'Mali: Islam, arms and money', in Morten Bøås and Kevin C. Dunn (eds), *Africa's Insurgents: Navigating an evolving landscape*, Boulder, CO: Lynne Rienner.

Bøås, Morten (2018) 'Militært bidrag uten debatt', *Dagbladet*, 27 February.

Bøås, Morten and Kevin C. Dunn (2013) *The Politics of Origin in Africa: Autochthony, citizenship and conflict*, London: Zed Books.

Bøås, Morten and Liv Elin Torheim (2013) 'The trouble in Mali – corruption, collusion, resistance', *Third World Quarterly*, vol. 34, no. 7, pp. 1279–92.

Bratton, Michael, Massa Coulibaly and Fabiana Machado (2002) 'Popular views on the legitimacy of the state in Mali', *Canadian Journal of African Studies*, vol. 36, no. 2, pp. 197–238.

Carbonnel, Alissa de and Robin Emmott (2018) 'Donors pledge $500 million more for troops in West Africa's Sahel', Reuters, 23rd February.

Cissé, Abdoul W., Ambroise Dakouo, Morten Bøås and Frida Kvamme (2017) *Perceptions about the EU Crisis Responses in Mali: A summary of perception studies*, EUN-PACK Policy Brief 7.7, Brussels.

Danish Demining Group (2014) *Evaluations des Risques Sécuritaires aux Frontiérs: Région du Liptako-Gourma: Mali, Burkina Faso et Niger*, Copenhagen: DDG.

Debos, Marielle (2009) *Porous Borders and Fluid Loyalties: Patterns of conflict in Darfur, Chad and the CAR*, New York: Center for Strategic and International Studies (CSIS).

Eriksen, Stein Sundstøl (2011) 'State failure in theory and practice: The idea of the state and contradiction of state formation', *Review of International Studies*, vol. 37, no. 1, pp 229–47.

European Parliament (2016), EU-Mauritania Fisheries Agreement: New Protocol, Brussels/Strasbourg: European Parliament.

Fjeldstad, Odd Helge, Morten Bøås, Julie B. Bjørkheim and Frida M. Kvamme (2018) *Building Tax Systems in Fragile States: Challenges, achievements and policy recommendations*, Bergen: CMI.

Flood, Derek Henry (2012) 'Between Islamization and secession: The contest for northern Mali', *CTC Sentinel*, vol. 5, no. 7, pp. 1–5.

Guichaoua, Yvan (2011) 'Circumstantial alliances and loose loyalties in rebellion making: The case of Tuareg insurgency in northern Niger (2007–2009)', in Yvan Guichaoua (ed.), *Understanding Collective Political Violence*, Basingstoke: Palgrave Macmillan.

Hesseling, Gerti and Han van Dijk (2005) 'Administrative decentralisation and political conflict in Mali', in Patrick Chabal, Ulf Engel and Anna-Maria Gentili (eds), *Is Violence Inevitable in Africa? Theories of conflict and approaches to conflict prevention*, Leiden: Brill.

ICG (2017) *The Social Roots of Jihadist Violence in Burkina Faso's North*, Brussels: ICG.

Keenan, Jeremy (2014) 'Interview', *Middle East Eye*, 30 June.

Marchal, Roland (2013) 'Une nouvelle aventure militaire au Sahara?' *SciencesPo Newsletter*, 4 February.

Marchesin, Philippe (1992) *Tribus, Ethnies et Pouvoir et Mauritanie*, Paris: Karthala.

Molenaar, Fransje (2017) *Irregular Migration and Human Smuggling Networks in Niger*, The Hague: Clingendael.

McDougall, Anne E. (2005) 'The legacy of slavery: Between discourse and reality', *Cahiers d'Études Africaines*, vol. 45, no. 179/80, pp. 957–86.

N'Diaye, Boubacar (2006) 'Mauritania, August 2005: Justice and democracy, or just another coup?', *African Affairs*, vol. 105, no. 420, pp. 421–41.

Penny, Joe (2018) 'Drones in the Sahara: A massive US drone base could destabilize Niger – and may even be illegal under its constitution', *The Intercept*, 18 February.

Potter, Geoff D. (2018) 'The renewed jihadi terror threat to Mauritania', *CTC Sentinel*, August, pp. 16–20.

Raineri, Luca (2018) 'Human smuggling across Niger: State-sponsored protection rackets and contradictory security imperatives', *Journal of Modern African Studies*, vol. 56, no. 1, pp. 63–86.

Raineri, Luca and Francesco Strazzari (2015) 'State, secession and jihad: The micropolitical economy of conflict in northern Mali', *African Security*, vol. 8, no. 4, pp. 249–71.

Raleigh, Clionadh and Caitriona Dowd (2013) 'Governance and conflict in the Sahel's ungoverned space', *Stability*, vol. 2, no. 2, pp. 1–17.

Rupesinghe, Natasja and Morten Bøås (2018) *Local Drivers of Violent Extremism in Central Mali*, Policy Brief, Addis Ababa: UNDP.

Sahlins, Marshall D. (1963) 'Poor man, rich man, big man, chief: Political types in Melanesia and Polynesia', *Comparative Studies in Society and History*, vol. 5, pp. 285–303.

Sangary, Boukary (2016) 'Le centre du Mali: epicentre du djihadisme?', *GRIP*, 20 May, pp. 1–12.

Scheele, Judith (2009) 'Tribus, états et fraude: al région frontalière algéro-malienne', *Etudes Rurales*, vol. 184, no. 2, pp. 79–94.

Seely, Jennifer (2001) 'A political analysis of decentralisation: Co-opting the Tuareg threat in Mali', *Journal of Modern African Studies*, vol. 39, no. 3, pp. 499–524.

Strazzari, Francesco (2014) 'Captured or capturing? Narcotics and political instability along the African route to Europe', *European Review of Organised Crime*, vol. 1, no. 2, pp. 5–34.

Strazzari, Francesco (2018) Ansarul Islam – the anatomy of an insurgency (unpublished draft).

Tardy, Thierry (2016) 'France: The unlikely return to UN peacekeeping', *International Peacekeeping*, vol. 23, no. 5, pp. 610–29.

Théroux-Benoni, Lori-Anne (2014) 'The long path to MINUSMA: Assessing the international response to the crisis in Mali', in Marco Wyss and Thierry Tardy (eds), *Peacekeeping in Africa: The evolving security architecture*, London: Routledge.

Tinti, Peter and Tom Westcott (2016) *The Niger–Libya Corridor: Smugglers' perspectives*, ISS Paper 299, Dakar.

UNDP (2017) *Human Development Report 2016: Human development for everyone*, New York: UNDP.

UNHCR (1991) *Mauritania: Country report*, New York: UNHCR.

Ursu, Anca-Elena (2018) *Under the Gun: Resource conflicts and embattled traditional authorities in central Mali*, The Hague: Clingendael – Netherlands Institute of International Relations.

Vium, Christian (2013) 'The phantom menace: Fear, rumours and the elusive presence of AQIM in south-eastern Mauritania', in Morten Bøås and Mats Utas (eds), 'Post-Gaddafi repercussions in the Sahel and West Africa', special section of the *Strategic Review for Southern Africa*, vol. 35, no. 2, pp. 92–116.

Wedel, Janine R. (2009) *Shadow Elite: How the world's new power brokers undermine democracy, government and the free market*, New York: Basic Books.

World Bank (2016a) *Mali – Population Data*, Washington, DC: World Bank.

World Bank (2016b) *Mauritania Overview*, Washington, DC: World Bank.

Index

About the author

Morten Bøås (PhD) is Research Professor at the Norwegian Institute of International Affairs (NUPI). He works predominantly on issues concerning peace and conflict in Africa, including issues such as land rights and citizenship conflicts, youths, ex-combatants and the new landscape of insurgencies and geopolitics.

Bøås has authored, co-authored and co-edited several books and published a number of articles for academic journals. He has conducted in-depth fieldwork in a number of African countries and travelled widely elsewhere on the continent. Listed below is a selection of his latest publications:

- Morten Bøås, co-author (2019). *Mali's Religious Leaders and the 2018 Presidential Elections*; Norsk Utenrikspolitisk Institutt; Oslo, 2019.

- Morten Bøås, co-author (2019). *A conflict-sensitive unpacking of the eu comprehensive approach to conflict and crisis mechanisms;* EUNPACK Executive Summary of the Final Report & Selected Policy Recommendations; Norsk Utenrikspolitisk Institutt; Oslo, 2019.

- Morten Bøås, co-author (2019). *Islamic Insurgents in the MENA Region. Global Threat or Regional Menace?;* NUPI Working Paper 884; Norsk Utenrikspolitisk Institutt; Oslo, 2019.

- Morten Bøås, co-author (2018). *Building tax systems in fragile states. Challenges, achievements and policy recommendations;* CMI Report 2018:3; Christian Michelsen Institute (CMI); Bergen, Norway, 2018.

- Morten Bøås, author (2018). *Rival priorities in the Sahel : finding the balance between security and development;* NAI Policy Notes; Uppsala, Sweden, 2018.

- Morten Bøås, editor (2018). *Comparing the EU's Output Effectiveness in the Cases of Afghanistan, Iraq and Mali;* Working Paper; Freie Universität, Berlin, 2018.

- Morten Bøås, author (2018). *New war zones or evolving modes of insurgency warfare?;* Chapter in Handbook of Political Anthropology; Edward Elgar Publishing, Cheltenham, UK, 2018

- Morten Bøås, co-author (2018). *The EU, security sector reform and border management in Mali.* Working paper on the implementation of EU crisis response in Mali.

- Morten Bøås, co-author (2018). *Pathways to Reconciliation in Divided Societies: Islamist Groups in Lebanon and Mali.*

About the Policy Dialogue Series

The Nordic Africa Institute Policy Dialogue Series is intended for strategists, analysts and decision-makers in foreign policy, aid and development. It aims to inform decision-making and the public debate.

The Policy Dialogue publications are generally written by researchers and based on their original research, but can also include contributions from experts and analysts with a perspective from outside the academic world. The opinions expressed are those of the authors and do not necessarily reflect the views of the Institute.

The series aims to offer a deepened understanding of a current topic, with an explicit purpose of giving policy relevant advice.

A list of previous titles in the Policy Dialogue Series can be found below:

1. HAVNEVIK, K., BRYCESON, D., BIRGEGÅRD, L.-E., MATONDI, P., & BEYENE, A. (2007). African Agriculture and The World Bank : Development or Impoverishment?

2. ZACK-WILLIAMS, A., & CHERU, F. (2008). The quest for sustainable development and peace : the 2007 Sierra Leone elections.

3. UTAS, M., PERSSON, M., & COULTER, C. (2008). Young female fighters in African wars : conflict and its consequences.

4. UTAS, M. (2009). Sexual abuse survivors and the complex of traditional healing : (G)local prospects in the aftermath of an African war.

5. ERIKSSON BAAZ, M., & STERN, M. (2011). La complexité de la violence : Analyse critique des violences sexuelles en République Démocratique du Congo (RDC).

6. VOGIAZIDES, L. (2012). 'Legal Empowerment of the Poor' versus 'Right to the City' : Implications for access to housing in urban Africa.

7. VAINIO, A. (2012). Market-based and Rights-based Approaches to the Informal Economy : A comparative analysis of the policy implications.

8. ERIKSSON BAAZ, M., & UTAS, M. (Eds.). (2012). Beyond "Gender and Stir" : Reflections on gender and SSR in the aftermath of African conflicts.

9. GELOT, L., & DE CONING, C. (Eds.). (2012). Supporting African peace operations.

10. NLANDU MAYAMBA MBUYA, T. (2013). Building a Police Force 'for the good' in DR Congo : Questions that still haunt reformers and reform beneficiaries.

11. FOLLÉR, M.-L., HAUG, C., KNUTSSON, B., & THÖRN, H. (2013). Who is responsible? : Donor-civil society partnerships and the case of hiv/aids work.

12. ADETULA, V. A. O., BEREKETEAB, R., & JAIYEBO, O. (2016). Regional economic communities and peacebuilding in Africa : the experiences of ECOWAS and IGAD.

13. BEREKETEAB, R. (2019). The Ethiopia-Eritrea Rapprochment : Peace and Stability in the Horn of Africa.

14. AEBY, M. (2019). SADC – The Southern Arrested Development Community?

⦿ OPEN ACCESS

All titles can be downloaded in full text for open access. Please visit NAI's online research publication database DiVA at http://nai.diva-portal.org.

www.ingramcontent.com/pod-product-compliance
Lightning Source LLC
Chambersburg PA
CBHW060829270326
41931CB00003B/107